Consciousness: A Primer

essays in search of their source

Gordon Phinn   (2019)

Contents

Consciousness: A Primer 7
What Is Consciousness? 11
Why Consciousness? 14
Consciousness Exploring Consciousness 17
Creating Form With Thought 21
Infinite Intelligence Shrinking Into an Ego .. 24
Where Does Consciousness Come from? 28
Three Cheers for Monism 36

"Consciousness comes first; it is the ground of all being. Everything else including matter, is a possibility of consciousness. And consciousness chooses out of these possibilities, all the events we experience."

Amit Goswami, the Quantum Doctor

"I had been vainly seeking a description of consciousness within science; instead, what I and others have to look for is a description of science within consciousness."

Amit Goswami, the Self Aware Universe

"Culture is a plot against the expansion of consciousness."

Terence McKenna

"Why our experiences with ET civilisations are a glimpse into a human future where the primary science will be Science of Consciousness."

Stephen Greer, Workshop (July 2018)

Consciousness: A Primer

So far, the bulk of my work has been to familiarize the reader with the attributes and potentials of astral consciousness, and to activate the understanding of their own astral bodies, that subtle level of the psyche which transcends both sleep and death, enabling the indwelling spirit to consciously experience as many areas of the astral planes as its innate curiosity will allow. Growth, by whatever method comes to hand, is always the goal.

The thrill of discovery that comes with the opening of astral experience can be almost overwhelming, and the excitement generated can easily extinguish whatever foothold has been established. Calmness is the key to continuation. To know and explore, however briefly, the landscapes and communities of the astral planes, recognize their unending magnificence and feel at home within it, is, in effect, to demolish the anxiety and doubt surrounding the spectre of mortality, freeing the spirit to soar and play.

That there exists and is accessible, other, more subtle areas beyond the heavens and paradises, transcending the promises of religions, is not a step everyone wishes to take. For many it seems pointless, a deliberate desecration of the perfect picnic. Having their fears and desires satisfied by the joys and pleasures of paradise seems like just what the doctor ordered for the aging body and weary spirit, so the proposed dissolution of the radiant and youthful post-mortem vehicle seems counterproductive, to say the least.

That thirst can be quenched, ambitions fulfilled and karma set aside for some bodiless passage through nothingness, with no culture, family, community or faith, seems quite incomprehensible, despite the occasional disappearance of friends in that direction. Almost as crazy as wanting to be born again into that horror show of life on earth.

Yet all mystical traditions have indicated that such realms not only exist, but are the source of all manifestation, from molecular structure to planetary orbits. As an inheritor and initiate of such esoteric teachings, I have hinted and suggested in many of my writings the utility of understanding the place of such realms in the overall hologram of life everlasting.

In this short series of essays I shall attempt to furnish the reader with a more complete conception of those formless energy planes, that ground of all being, that *void without form or substance*, the Unmanifest, the Godhead, that is our source and succour. I have been inspired to do so by the fairly recent embrace of the concept and role of consciousness in absorbing our interaction with aliens, their vehicles and seemingly magical technologies. When researchers like Grant Cameron, Richard Dolan, Stephen Greer, Linda Moulton Howe and Nick Redfern all allude to abductees being invited to pilot UFO's and being told to use their own thoughts to do so, as the 'saucers' are themselves sentient beings, responsive to mental energy, they are on the edge of seeing that all of us, - humans, aliens and sentient saucers - are the products of consciousness. As are the life streams of mineral, plant and elemental life, although I suspect it will be sometime yet before such researchers recognise thought responsive trees, emotionally sensitive plants, playful elves and magisterial devas, including them in their categories of fantasies now filed under "real". And although there are few indicators of our relationship to our "space" brothers in the esoteric traditions I humbly represent, they are sufficient to indicate the direction we should proceed in: that of willing and fearless embrace. And for that this is a primer.

What Is Consciousness?

I see the word all over these days. In studies of psychic abilities. In talks by UFO researchers. In meditation manuals. In neurology and quantum physics. In race relations. In psychedelic research. In animal rights organisations. In explorations of plant, vegetable and tree life. Its use has gone, as we say, viral.

Consciousness can be seen as *all that we are conscious of*. Through our thoughts, sense perceptions, emotions and intuitions. Of course, each individual, depending on their level of openness and acceptance, is conscious to a greater or lesser degree. As we grow in desire and ambition, we discover more and more in the world around us, more to be conscious of. And as we pursue those threads of interest, gathering knowledge and understanding as we go, and generally making use of that knowledge to better ourselves in one way or another, we come to a stage where consciousness would seem to be more than the objects, beings and systems that appear in our explorations.

At some point we may discover, as a theory, rumour or fantasy, that consciousness is much more than the driver of sentient beings, that it is, or could be, the actual life force itself, something beyond the molecular and sub-atomic particles that, through their bonding, allow perceptible forms to manifest.

Is consciousness the prime substance, the first cause, the ground of all being, the word of god spelling out the very idea of light, as in *let there be light*? For me the answer would be an unqualified yes. What animates me is what animates you is what makes plants grow horses gallop and fish swim, fires the suns that render planets habitable and charges the gravitational force that keeps us all in place.

You might say it was the original miracle worker, that god which moves in mysterious ways to make the plan unfold. You might let fear categorise it as an imprisoning force, that which gives us just enough energy to appreciate the cage in which we are contained. You could, just as easily, let it liberate your need to expand and encompass, to better know the energies in and around you.

As we explore consciousness, for immediate gain or long term growth, we slowly uncover its greatest secret: that everything, including emptiness, is constructed of consciousness, that even vacuums and voids have pertinent advice. And that advice is: keep going for you have no other choice. The end is not nigh, nor will it ever be. Creation and destruction are propelled through their cycles unceasingly and passengers can participate or decline any offer that time and space connive.

So listen to the trees, the rivers, the traffic, the celebrities, cultures and aliens, - they all have something to tell you about yourself and the illusions you cherish. The building blocks of one are the building blocks of the others. Patterns beguiling the perceiver of patterns, who herself is a product of ineffable patterns.

Why Consciousness?

Sounds like the annoyingly curious child going *why daddy*? every fifteen minutes and the parent attempting the impossible: explaining every shred of existence the wondering child puzzles over. But it is a questioning pose we all slip into eventually. Usually after the why floods, why tornadoes, why war, why pointless suffering, why ruthless evil and even why good guys finish last.

As a metaphysical quester of many lifetimes and playgrounds of incarnation, I am occasionally tempted take the plunge, part the waters of the mystery and walk through. And when I do, walk through that is, what I find on the other side, whether galactic or sub-atomic, is that which comes before energy and its manifestations. You know, energy which propels planets in their orbits and people in their preferences, that force which pushes you into action and then pressures you into rest.

The creative juice of the universes if you like. The mysterious drive behind the evolution of forms, mineral, vegetable and animal. That thing which keeps your fingernails and hair growing after you die.

That excitement which animates your refreshed or resurrected spirit once the fear of death has itself died. That pleasurable joy which finances your stay in the paradise of your choice. That fount of wisdom that seems so self evident when thought is unleashed from its belief systems. That immense power behind your many manifestations in this and other worlds. All those beings that are born of you, go about their business in time and space, and, as the blues song goes, bring it all back home to you.

Consciousness is what makes it all possible and renders it all useful. Useful for your education in the cosmic game of being and not-being. For even when you're absent from team practice, here on the planet, some other aspect of that greater you reigning over the family tree is here, hoisting its ego flag. Shouting *here I am love me*!

And when you're not here, but languishing in heaven, relearning what you thought you'd lost forever, you can look down and chuckle at all the marvellous silliness of egos shaping up to expectations, and know that it is consciousness that gives them the freedom to do so and you the freedom to watch them. You can present yourself above the torments, await the explosion and catch some startled falling soul like some falling star, and as the song says, put it in your pocket and save it for a rainy day.

Child's play in the pit of hell, yes, but just another day in the shadow play of consciousness.

Consciousness Exploring Consciousness

As we proceed on our inner journeys, employing whatever paths, traditional or innovative, that seem to fit our current needs—prayer, yoga, lucid dreaming, meditation, running, sacramental psychedelics, astral projection, remote viewing, teleportation—we arrive at the understanding that all is consciousness, - matter, thought, emotion - , that everything is alive and self-directed, self-aware organisms pushing the envelope of their potential.

When we arrive at this juncture it is often the fulfilment of teachings studied and practiced for years, concepts and theories that seemed to unravel the paradoxes and mysteries structuring the obstacle race that seems to constitute our lives. All those whys and hows uttered in frustration and resentment.

When our personal perceptions confirm the teachings we have studied and practiced there is usually a tremendous uplift of exhilaration that erupts in our hearts, or maybe charges down through our crown chakra, illuminating our earlier ignorance as some silly detour on the way to the destination that is here and now and always has been, had we not been distracted in some dalliance with the shiny baubles of temporary illusions.

That exhilaration, to be one with all that is, all the microbes, elementals, committees, transactions, beliefs, communities and tragedies, while invigorating to the aspirant, is almost commonplace for the archangel or adept, or any highly evolved being going about their business. To them we are like children in the playground who have found the gate in the fence is actually unlocked and the river beyond safely shallow and full of delightful little fish.

Our brief encounters with such cosmic consciousness are indeed a taste of the holy grail hinted at and sometimes promised in all the ancient teachings. Usually we cannot sustain the transcendence of self-consciousness for very long, such is the fragility of the new body built to experience it. It only gains strength and flexibility from repeated exposures to the bracing radiance that the elevation engenders. Our personal concerns and petty ambitions always reassert themselves with that familiar pride of attachment, anchoring our flight into the empyrean in the harbour of habit and neurosis.

But even these brief interludes in the line-up of tiresome commitments that claim our time can be enough to show us that we are at one with the consciousness that is endlessly creating and recreating the universe as it expands beyond any horizon we devise for it. For we, as incarnate experiments dreamed up by Monads making adjustments to earlier templates, are endlessly creating and re-creating ourselves in the various worlds available for the quenching of our thirsts. Those selves are never inactive, whether alive on the physical, alive on the astral or footloose and fancy free in the nirvanas of formless radiance, we never cease to participate in one fashion or another. Our slice of consciousness operates more or less exactly as the greater ones, like the fabled Anima Mundi, do, exploring expansion and contraction and self-replication in any manner perceived as possible.

All this can be experienced in moments of meditation, consciousness projection or psychedelic intoxication. How much of it can be absorbed and retained for further use depends on the flexibility of the fragile ego, who much prefers the habit of forgetfulness, where blame can be righteously apportioned and responsibility playfully shucked.

Why did no one tell us the gate was unlocked? What was all that stuff about the river being too deep and dragging the unwary out to sea? When will authority release us from bondage?

Why does society allow such injustice? What are you really doing god?

Creating Form with Thought

Communications from the astral plane always stress the creative power of thought, ranging from the unconscious streams confusing the recent arrival, causing them to flip from one scene to another as ghosts touring memories, sometimes flushed out by the cares of those they left behind and others fuelled by regrets, desires and vague anxieties bubbling to the surface, to the curious onlooker now settled to the post-mortem state who has been told that they can think little things into existence, -twigs, buttons, spoons – to the long-time resident who has refined the technique and can execute watercolours with the tip of her finger, construct elaborate furniture without hammer, saw or screw, design a room's interior with all flourishes and details in place, and then replace it all with another style the very next day.

And by the time a spirit can attach the long-time resident label to themselves they have likely heard, if not in fact witnessed, the magical construction of some elaborate institution such as a school, museum or plaza by a group of dead architects working in concert, that is by linking their minds and focusing their plans. And others will have been informed that the astral communities and landscapes in which they live and have their being were created long ago by higher spirits who were up to the task and saw the need.

Some communicators will point out that that power of conception in human minds, coupled with practicality and determination, is what brings forms into manifestation here on earth and thus it is the power of thought, in the guise of imagination, that ushers anything into manifestation, on any plane. To this I would add that the spirit planes were designed and manifested by those of us who'd volunteered for the project while the physical plane was yet unfit for habitation and we lived there quite contentedly as happy puppies in paradise until the earth was ready for some primitive frontier exploration.

The imagination, thought and implementation so far discussed are all tools that consciousness creates and then uses to explore the farther regions of its very own self. As people joke that God created fingers and opposable thumbs that we might be more useful to ourselves, so too does consciousness create the implements it requires for specific tasks. *We* are useful implements just as planets are useful testing grounds and spirit worlds are happy playgrounds.

Infinite Intelligence Shrinking Into an Ego

It happens all the time, just like birth and death, but it is something of a challenge to perceive with clarity. Most of the mystically inclined throughout what we call history would declare it invisible to normal sight, perhaps even to the newly activated third eye. A fully operating crown chakra would know, if it felt so inclined after interrogation by the ego, should the ego know that such questioning is possible for the aspirant, who may have heard that consciousness enters form without fanfare or forewarning but remains naive as to the tracking of each occurrence.

As it is, any number of sparks from the divine fire, that realm of the unmanifest beyond all paradises and heavens, take wing into the spheres of form, becoming something by entering the seed of a body, by encoding its dna, by blending its energy with the physical structure, by taking up residence in that all-too-fleeting house, by becoming the owner and enduring the obligations that come with such territory.

Leaving the infinite for a ride in limitation, becoming an "I" that immediately creates "the other", and all the little others which comprise it, forces us to shrink our immense understanding of all and everything into a tiny frame overwhelmed by fear, hunger and desire. The world of self and other: we all live there, breathing the same breath and hearing the same heartbeat, but our addresses conspire to separate us into dwellings distinct in their trifles. And as we dance through the details of our comedies and dramas, sparring with every new tune, we dive into the illusions that draw us onward into the suffering which moves us to seek solutions and escapes.

Those solutions are many: the comforts of love, the warmth of family, the fortress of money, the reach of status, the throne of pride, the purpose of ambition, the prize of success. All are temporary, all are fragile, all can collapse in a moment's contempt. And often do, despite our urgent stacking of safety measures. That urgency, that insistence, that determination to outsmart suffering, it does little but construct a series of shoddy shacks which misfortune can easily find and flood.

In our despair at being so decimated we can sour into resentment or sweeten into repair. Either way we learn the lesson that leapt up into our laps as we snoozed by the fire. Life lessons can make us loopy with anxiety and murderous with dread, all of it unpleasant and distasteful to the heart. And all of it is the inevitable result of creating an "I" to experience the world and its multitudes of others.

We enter the Game, knowing it will grind us down into a fine powder that will serve to imbue the waters of life with a pungent aroma that could only be us, an aromatic tincture that will be added to the menu the next time we choose to make a meal of ourselves.

*

When the "I" that is here, pretending to be me, looks back to the boy and before that the baby, and before that the spirit about to enter, and before that the being bouncing around the astral being love and foolish fun, and before that the Monad, the Atman, the all-knowing essence, supervising planets and seeding them with sparks, simultaneously a minor deity and an army of unknowing disciples, some smart, some stupid, some sniffing the breeze for clues, I see the unfolding of the great mystery of Being being something other than enigmatic, being more a pile of desires eating each other's shadows, all the while ignorant of the light which breeds that shadow, believing all is real when really it's not.

Where Does Consciousness Come From?

Consciousness does not arrive, out of breath and full of apologies. Nor does it leave, looking despondent and dusting off old explanations. Consciousness was here long before anyone realised it. Before galaxies, committees, dinosaurs, event horizons, religions, export tariffs and microbes. Just as the spirit worlds are heavily populated by spirits of all cultures and races long before you, in your grieving, turn to acknowledge and explore their existence and purpose.

Often labelled *God* by those who would bow in deference, sometimes the *Great Spirit*, others the presence of *All That Is*, and yet others the *Universal Creativity* that endlessly manifests all the products and services in which we become entangled, and sometimes the current paradigm surfaces to be encountered, *Consciousness,* and as Richard Smoley subtitles his book "The Dice Game

Of Shiva", *how consciousness creates the universe*, we have a prime example of the new metaphor describing the old idea. Old wine in new bottles as the saying goes.

There are many ways to make the fluctuations and paradoxes of consciousness more palatable to our refined and cultured attitudes. Denial and ignorance are often employed. Explaining it all away remains a popular choice. Leaving it to experts and authorities can be an easy out. Blaming the unrestrained and ruthless greed that capitalism fosters and then deploys is undoubtedly fashionable and will win you many friends. Yet consciousness recognises no boundaries, moralities, beliefs or faiths. Even more than that sun who shines on everyone regardless of moral probity, consciousness feeds every creative activity, every push to expand or ruin. Using mother nature as its utensil it creates and destroys with equal ease. Compassion and mercy are absent from its playbook. The energies of fire and water, for example, are free to do as they please. We learn to respect their unleashed powers, because in truth we have little option.

Like our centuries spent fearing a vengeful God and his earthly enforcers, when we thought we had no choice, we now structure that behaviour around the whims of nature, laughing only when our shelters prove adequate protection. Although we are ourselves active elements of consciousness we have learned to dance around the other elements which threaten our safety and stability. The growth of our problem solving intellects has enabled our escape from the protective shield of religion but left us worshipping the amoral cleverness of science, which has the remarkable ability to solve one problem while creating three more. God has been deposed from King Supreme, Designer-in-Chief to something along the lines of fitness trainer and yoga instructor, while the protocols and products of science are mindlessly praised by its own practitioners, signatories to an unspoken treaty hidden from view and thus the fundamentalist materialism from which it springs remains mostly unchallenged.

After decades of poking and prodding the brain, neurologists have yet to uncover the method by which consciousness arises from that maze of chemical and electrical interactions, but because their assumptions are materially based, – that matter is all that exists, – they continue to hope that organs like the brain will finally give up their secrets, just as soon as the right experiment is readied and tested. Not unlike religionists who continually refer to their ancient sacred texts, hoping that fresh interpretation will unleash the divine mystery from its hiding place. Philosophers call it the "mind-body problem" and continue to circle about it cleverly and hopelessly. How on earth does the brain produce consciousness? Wrong question. The right question: how does consciousness produce the brain? The same way it produces retinas, tornadoes, butterflies, barcodes and fleeting glimpses: the magical art of manifestation. The same alchemy we practice, with a little help from our friends, when we weigh anchor in the astral and set sail for that precious womb where our cruise with wonder and wounds continues. All very mystical admittedly and completely unfit for the testing that hypotheses undergo and yet, remarkably, replicated every other second around the planet.

Richard Smoley quotes philosopher Colin McGinn, who argues that "the problem of consciousness is fundamentally insoluble" and has been accused by his colleagues of "Mysterianism". And hey, I agree. Yet despite the many esoteric teachings from various traditions, like the Kabbalah, Hermeticism, Hindu mythology, esoteric Buddhism and 'hidden' Christianity that I might quote from, there is no intellectually satisfying argument to be persuaded by. There are myths, legends, assertions and metaphors, carefully couched in mystical texts, but there are no proofs and likely never will be. Our science addled brains cannot compute that which cannot be diced and analysed, regardless of how refined the arguments become.

The mystery can only be encountered and experienced by enquiring spirits surrendering to the unknown. Psychedelics, meditation and out of body experience are three paths I would recommend. With psychedelics you can understand how the brain shapes perceptions, but that which is perceived, however relentlessly changing shape and texture, has an independent existence and has been created elsewhere. Later, in the same experience, you can experience the calm, radiant ocean of light that many others have reported, calling it the Godhead or the Ground of all Being from which all things emerge. When you are there you will have no doubt about its functioning reality, because you have emerged from arguing polarities and intellectual doubt and have entered the oneness that is beyond speculation. Juts as healing is not curing, knowing is not proving.

With meditation you can move in much the same direction but without all the fireworks. The contents of your brain, the thoughts, regrets, anxieties and fantasies, will parade themselves before you, trying to tempt you into attachment, acting out their pathos and drama like children at bedtime. Waves of emotions will wash over you, trying much the same thing. First hint: the observer to all this is not the brain or the personality. You are more the sky in which these clouds pass. And as we know, that brilliant blue is but a pretty illusion leading to the enormity of star-studded blackness beyond. Later, minutes or months later, you will come to rest beyond all this activity and experience *the peace which passeth all understanding*, and while being unable to explain it to your friends, will know that this subdued bliss is where you belong.

With out of body experience, you can find yourself inspecting your bedroom, your garden, your neighbourhood, earthbound ghosts, other projectors, the various astral planes, hellish and heavenly, your dead loved ones, and eventually the formless energy planes, that Godhead again, beyond all activity. But such is the entrancement of all this freedom and beguiling beauty, it might be quite some 'time' before you get there. The joys of flight, family reunion, breath-taking beauty and those faces so familiar from past adventures can easily enthrall the exploring psyche, showing you how to hide your holy grail from your desiring self.

Will such attainment become more common as we evolve? I suspect so. Those of us who have freed themselves from the constraints of religion and autocratic society certainly have a head start, and hopefully our brave explorations will inspire others in less salubrious surroundings. And let's face it, there's no lack of those. Each of those paths I have outlined can lead to an immersion in the ocean of nothingness that is the *Godhead* spoken of in mystical texts and only personal experience, not any persuasive tactics, will convince. That those explorations may one day be aided by technological innovations I have no doubt. A computer program that mimics the magically morphing patterns of psychedelics, allowing entry and enthrallment? An energy beam that projects you beyond all heavens to the *Ground of All Being*, perhaps similar to the portals that now transfer staff from Earth to the Moon and Mars? All of this is possible and I would say likely. Researchers like Stephen Greer hint that similar innovations have already been tested in what is known as 'unacknowledged special access programs' and have been kept under tight wraps for decades lest they be weaponised, or more importantly, render conventional energy systems redundant. Other experiencers have encountered military personnel out of body but still in service to their contractual ideals, suggesting that they have been carefully trained to exit and explore.

But honestly, how many of us would be ready to abandon the heavens and paradises for a taste of formless bliss in which radiant bodies, personal identities, pleasures and joys are notably absent? And who of us, thus enabled, would be able to convince others that we know the source from which consciousness arises? And do so gently, without the passions that power coercion and conversion?

We'd say, *Yeah, it's all too much, but you really have to check it out for yourself.*

Really, go to nowhere, be nobody, get all charged up and then return, blissed to the max but understanding nothing?

And we'd say, *Yeah.*

Three Cheers for Monism

Yes, all the above can be read as Three Cheers for Monism! In the debates throughout the centuries over spirit vs. matter, both philosophical and theological, the accepted dualism served religions' agendas well, sourcing all its good vs. evil directives that funneled the faithful into the heaven or hell bound channels. Philosophers seemed to prefer the mind/body dualism with its current neurologists' reboot, the mind/brain fracas.

Of course, all dualisms emerge from the One as soon as we do, leaving the radiant void, the ground of all being, to become a little being getting buffeted about by those slings and arrows of outrageous fortune. Suddenly, with a form to rally round, it's the self and the other, the warm and the cold, the male and the female, the right and the wrong. the eat or be eaten, the good guys and the bad guys, the good and the evil. They are all as inevitable and unavoidable as sun and shadow.

Wikipedia asserts three types of monism, – priority monism, existence monism and substance monism. Substance monism posits "that only one kind of stuff exists, although many things may be made up of this stuff". And although existence monism has a lot going for it ("there exists only a single thing, which can only be arbitrarily divided into many things"), aligning itself with one of my old favourites, Neo-Platonism, ("everything is derived from The One"), for me substance monism wins by a nose.

It's becoming a new age commonplace to say that we are, by our continued efforts, spiritualizing matter, and I'd be inclined to agree. That matter is completely malleable when directed by thought on the astral plane is obvious to experiencers and those who take the time to collate their reports and evaluate them. And as the physical plane's vibration is gradually raised to that of the astral, such miraculous activity will veer toward the norm, the norm that is accepted and almost forgotten, and *that,* my friends, is spiritualising matter.

How long that process will take to come to some kind of fruition is anyone's guess, depending, I suspect, on how many of us will resist it, albeit unconsciously, but given the now regular occurrence of trips to heaven and back, courtesy of the nde, and that benign invasion of the orbs into our visual field and that of our digital recorders, I would venture sooner rather than later.

I see the term Monism was introduced by Christian Von Wolff in "Logic" (1728), to "designate types of philosophical thought in which the attempt was made to eliminate the dichotomy of body and mind and explain all phenomena by one unifying principle" and that monism lost popularity due to the emergence of analytic philosophy in the 20th century, and whose chief proponents ridiculed the whole question as "incoherent mysticism".

Transcendental experience is often incoherent to those who study with a logical and analytical bent. But to those who surrender to the experience, casting off their safety nets and crutches with glee, that apparent incoherence is transformed. Transformed beyond a higher level of order into game playing gestures commensurate with giggling.

That's the cosmic giggle, the one that mocks our strivings and attachments, urging us to sing and let go as we drift in the winds of life. That's the crazy wisdom that unhinged teachers teach. If you meet the Buddha on the road, give him your mirror.

*

Consciousness: A Primer

is published by *mooninjoon* 2019

Gordon Phinn reserves the moral right

to be known as the author of this work.

*

mooninjoon, Oakville, Ontario, Canada

Printed in Great Britain
by Amazon